# HORRiD HENRY'S
## Guide to
# Perfect Parents

# HORRID HENRY'S
## Guide to
## Perfect Parents

Francesca Simon
*Illustrated by* Tony Ross

Orion
Children's Books

First published in Great Britain in 2013
by Orion Children's Books
a division of the Orion Publishing Group Ltd
Orion House
5 Upper Saint Martin's Lane
London WC2H 9EA
An Hachette UK Company

1 3 5 7 9 10 8 6 4 2

Text © Francesca Simon 2013
Illustrations © Tony Ross 2013

The Orion Publishing Group's policy is to use papers that
are natural, renewable and recyclable products and made
from wood grown in sustainable forests. The logging and
manufacturing processes are expected to conform to the
environmental regulations of the country of origin.

A catalogue record for this book is available
from the British Library.

Printed in Great Britain

ISBN 978 1 4440 0905 7

www.horridhenry.co.uk
www.orionbooks.co.uk

*For Josh,*
*who trained me so well.*

# URGENT!!
# URGENT!!!

### Calling all Purple Hand
### Gang Members!

I happened to sneak into my parents'
bedroom to find out where they'd
hidden my birthday presents and see
if I'd *finally* be getting a Blaster Buzzer
for my birthday (still NO. It's so
unfair!)

Well, I didn't find any hidden presents. But I did find a book. Not just any book. A horrible book. A deadly, scary, poisonous book. A book that should be banned everywhere in the universe. A book so awful and so horrid that any parent caught reading it should be locked up in prison and forced to watch *Name that Vegetable* and *Daffy and her Dancing Daisies* 24 hours a day.

And what was this evil book?

# BE THE BOSS!

Top Tips
for
Kid
Control

Can you believe it? My mean, horrible parents have been trying to ... to ... tame me! How could they be so horrid? Well no way. Because not only do I now know *all* their parenting tricks, but I'm going to turn the tables on them with my Top Tips for ...

... Parent Control!!! Yes!

This book will teach you everything you need to know about training your parents. After all, who's the boss? You? Or them? Too right, you. And don't let them forget it. It's hard, heavy work training perfect parents, but do it right and it will be worth it.

So here are my top secret parent-taming tips. Hide this book from prying eyes, including tell-tale little brothers and sisters. It's your secret weapon. And oh yeah, I know you'll thank me forever, but words are cheap. All donations gratefully received.

# Perfect Parents

# By Henry

Perfect parents let you do whatever you want, whenever you want.

They let you decide what's for dinner, never make you eat vegetables, and give you control of the TV remote.

But how, I hear you scream, can you turn your mean, horrible, bossy parents into perfect ones? Just follow my simple training tips.

# Shame and Tame

Remind your parents daily how marvellous your friends' parents are. Sighing loudly and saying, "I wish I had Ralph's parents. They always let him stay up late/eat as many sweets as he wants/watch loads of TV etc."

Other great phrases
to shame and tame parents:
"Margaret's parents gave *her*
a Demon Dagger Sabre."

"Josh's parents let *him* pour
his own chocolate sauce."

"Gurinder's parents give loads more pocket money than you."

"Susan's parents let her play on the computer for as long as she likes."

Telling them how wonderful other parents are will make them want to shape up fast.

# Praise good behaviour

No one likes being told off
all the time. Even parents.

So remember gang, when they give you those extra sweets you deserve, or let you watch extra TV, *PRAISE* their good behaviour. You want to make them do this all the time. Parents want praise and attention, so give it to them.

Trust me, they'll be rushing to stuff extra desserts into you, and letting you off your chores.

Speaking of chores…

# How to make your parents do your chores for you

make the bed
Dust the cat
wash the dishes
wash Peter
Clean Bedroom
Oil my bike
tidy the kitchen Cupboard
Hoover the crumbs out
of settee

What are you, a slave?
How dare parents ask you to help
around the house. Don't you have
enough to do as it is?

Have you ever heard that phrase, "If you want something done well, do it yourself?" Parents know this is true, so your goal is to do all chores so slowly, and so badly, and so ungraciously, and with so much wailing and gnashing and groaning and moaning and sighing, that your parents will give up and yell: "Oh, all right, I'll do it myself."

Victory!
Congratulations!
You are now well on your way to
having perfectly trained parents.

Pssst. Some parents will take longer
to crack than others. Some of you
will have to work for weeks, months,
maybe even years. But trust me.
They will all give up eventually.

# Tantrums

All parents have tantrums.
They yell and scream when they
don't get their way (ie. when *you* don't
do what *they* want.)
Just remember, you'd have tantrums
too if you were old and wrinkly
like them.

My advice is, stay calm.
Suggest your parent has time out.
If you are really an expert parent
tamer, urge them to sit on the
naughty step until they calm down.

Of course, tantrums are also *your* secret weapon. For some reason, parents usually only have tantrums when no one else is looking. Bah! Tantrums are best staged in public, or just before your parents have to go somewhere important, or when guests are over. Believe me they'll promise you anything if you'll only just STOP screaming.

# Money

You want it.

They have it.

It's so unfair.

Why do parents have so much more money than you do?

Wouldn't it be great if you could have all the cash, and give *them* pocket money?

Well, when I'm King that's exactly what will happen.

Till then, you just have to try and get as much money as you can by making your parents feel guilty.

1. Tell them everyone gets loads more pocket money than you do. (See page 16).

2. Remind them of all the things you *need* to buy.

3. Point out that they can't expect any presents from you if they give you so little money.

4. Tell them you need to practice money management skills and you can't on the pitiful amount they give you.

5. If all else fails . . .
tell them it's time for a raise.

Sadly, there are always things that you want that for some reason parents don't want you to have.

For example, Roller Bowlers, the world's best trainers, the shoes on wheels you can set to

Screech

Fire-engine

Drums

Cannon

Siren

and Sonic Boom.

They are so loud you can hear them from miles off!

Wow!

So, how do you make them buy you great stuff like that? You BORE and NAG them to death. Just go on and on and on about them. Believe me they will eventually give in just to keep you quiet. Then don't forget, PRAISE GOOD BEHAVIOUR. Warning: Be careful! If you're watching TV, and see an ad for something you want, don't nag them instantly, or your mean, horrible parents might decide that you're watching too much telly.
Just wait a little bit to be safe.

# How to get the food you want

One word – allergies.
I know *I'm* allergic to fruit, vegetables, soup, salad, and muesli.

In fact, the only food I can eat is chocolate, cake, crisps, burgers, pizza and sweets.

# T.V.

Remember the magic word?
No, it's not please, it's *homework*.

You'd be amazed how much TV you can watch by saying it's for homework.

Parents like to feel they are helping their children in school, so what better way to help than to let kids watch "educational" programmes like *Terminator Gladiator*, *Mutant Max*, and *Hog House* (tee hee).

# Bedtime

Always tricky. Parents want you in bed as early as possible. You, of course, want to stay up as late as possible. So if your bedtime is 8 o'clock, here are some parent-training tips to get that extra time you deserve. One is sure to work!

1. Tell them everyone gets to stay up later than you do.

2. Delay bedtime for as long
as possible.

See how slowly you can brush
your teeth. Drag your feet as you
stagger up the stairs to your bedroom.

Take hours putting on your pyjamas.
Say you need to do your homework.
Ask for endless drinks of water.
Once in bed, keep coming downstairs.
Any excuse will do.

3. Once you have tormented them sufficiently, promise that if they let you stay up an hour later, you'll go to bed with no fuss. (Then keep your word, and your parents will learn that they can spend an hour struggling to heave you into bed at 8, or have a quiet evening with no fuss and stress and argument. The well-trained parent will make the right choice!)

(See pages 19 to 22 on rewarding good behaviour if you need extra practice).

# Congratulations

Well done!
You are now the proud owner of
perfectly trained and tamed parents.
You call the shots, as you lounge
around eating chocolates and guzzling
Fizzywizz drinks while your perfect
parents wait on you hand and foot,
eager to do whatever–

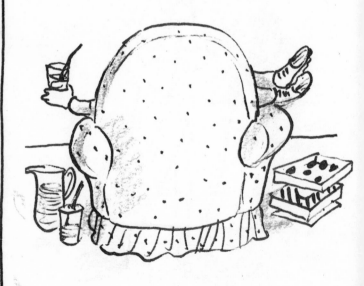

Wait, what's that you're saying?
You did everything I told you,
and they *aren't* tamed? Well, there's
only one possible explantion . . .

Your parents have read this book,
and armed themselves against
your weasel words.

# You didn't hide it well enough! Ninnyhammer.

I did warn you, this information is top secret, how could you let your parents get hold of this book, now they'll know exactly how to–

Come to think of it, I wonder if that's why my parents seem to be resisting their training…

# Oops.

# Collect all the
# Horrid Henry storybooks!

Horrid Henry

Horrid Henry
and the Secret Club

Horrid Henry Tricks
the Tooth Fairy

Horrid Henry
Gets Rich Quick

Horrid Henry's Nits

Horrid Henry's
Haunted House

Horrid Henry and
the Mummy's Curse

Horrid Henry's
Revenge

Horrid Henry and the
Bogey Babysitter

Horrid Henry's Stinkbomb

Don't miss the
**BRAND NEW**
**HORRiD HENRY**
storybook,

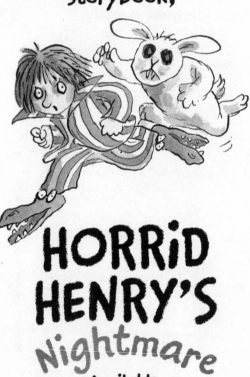

**HORRiD**
**HENRY'S**
**Nightmare**

Available
from June 2013

Visit my wicked website
www.horridhenry.co.uk
for jokes, book news,
competitions and more!

Don't forget
to sign up for my
**newsletter** while
you're there!

www.horridhenry.co.uk

# BOOKs rock!

## Want to read more?

### VISIT your local bookshop

- Get great recommendations for books you'll love
- Meet your favourite authors & illustrators at brilliant events
- Discover books you never knew existed!

 www.booksellers.org.uk/bookshopsearch

### JOIN your local library

You can browse and borrow from a huge selection of book and get recommendations of what to read next from expert librarians – all for FREE!

You can also discover libraries' wonderful children's and family readi activities – such as reading groups (see www.chatterbooks.org.uk), author events and challenges (see www.summerreadingchallenge.org.u

## Get Online

Explore www.worldbookday.com to discover a world of bonkersly brilliant beautiful books!

- Downloads and activities for your favourite books and authors
- Cool games, trailers and videos
- Fantastic competitions
- Author events in your area
- Sign up for the **FREE** monthly e-newsletter

*And much, much more...*

# Win!

# £100 of BOOKS
## each for *you* and
## *your school*!

## All you have to do is answer one
## VERY important question.

Imagine you're travelling to a *far away planet*, or a *desert island*, or even a *desert* ... and, wherever you're going, there are **NO BOOKS**. Luckily, you're allowed to take just **ONE** book with you on your journey. What would it be?

For your chance to **WIN**, just tell us
the name of your chosen book!

To enter go to **www.worldbookday.com**

# the
# orion star

Sign up for **the orion star**
newsletter to get inside information
about your favourite children's authors
as well as exclusive competitions and
early reading copy giveaways.

**www.orionbooks.co.uk/newsletters**

Follow  on

Orion
Children's Books